Contents

D0069357

Venus is a **planet** named after the **Roman goddess** of love and beauty.

EXPLORING SPACE

Venus

by Colleen Sexton

Consultant:
Duane Quam, M.S. Physics
Chair, Minnesota State
Academic Science Standards
Writing Committee

Note to Librarians, Teachers, and Parents:

Blastoff! Readers are carefully developed by literacy experts and combine standards-based content with developmentally appropriate text.

Level 1 provides the most support through repetition of high-frequency words, light text, predictable sentence patterns, and strong visual support.

Level 2 offers early readers a bit more challenge through varied simple sentences, increased text load, and less repetition of high-frequency words.

Level 3 advances early-fluent readers toward fluency through increased text and concept load, less reliance on visuals, longer sentences, and more literary language.

Level 4 builds reading stamina by providing more text per page, increased use of punctuation, greater variation in sentence patterns, and increasingly challenging vocabulary.

Level 5 encourages children to move from "learning to read" to "reading to learn" by providing even more text, varied writing styles, and less familiar topics.

Whichever book is right for your reader, Blastoff! Readers are the perfect books to build confidence and encourage a love of reading that will last a lifetime!

This edition first published in 2016 by Bellwether Media, Inc.

No part of this publication may be reproduced in whole or in part without written permission of the publisher. For information regarding permission, write to Bellwether Media, Inc., Attention: Permissions Department, 6012 Blue Circle Dr., Minnetonka, MN 55343.

Library of Congress Cataloging-in-Publication Data

Sexton, Colleen A., 1967-
Venus / by Colleen Sexton.
   p. cm. – (Blastoff! readers. Exploring space)
Includes bibliographical references and index.
Summary: "Introductory text and full-color images explore the physical characteristics of Venus in space. Intended for students in kindergarten through third grade"–Provided by publisher.
ISBN: 978-1-60014-403-5 (hardcover : alk. paper)
ISBN: 978-1-60014-685-5 (paperback : alk. paper)
1. Venus (Planet)–Juvenile literature. I. Title.
QB621.S49 2010
523.42–dc22   2009037989

Venus can be seen from Earth. It shines brightly in the evening sky.

Venus

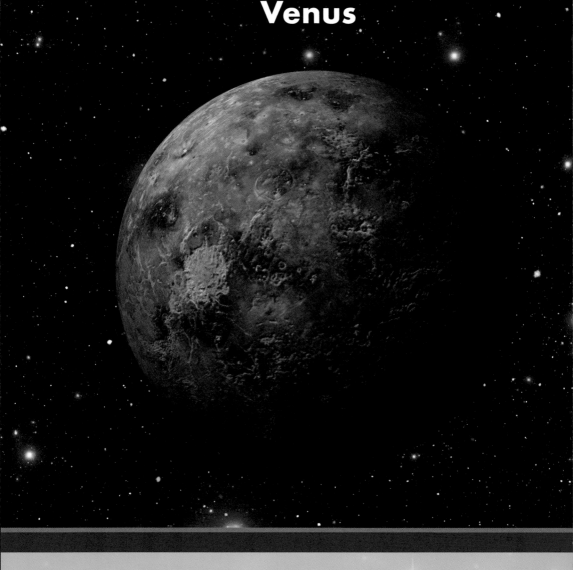

Venus is called Earth's twin. Venus and Earth are closer together than any other two planets.

Earth

Venus and Earth are almost the same size. Venus is about 7,520 miles (12,100 kilometers) wide.

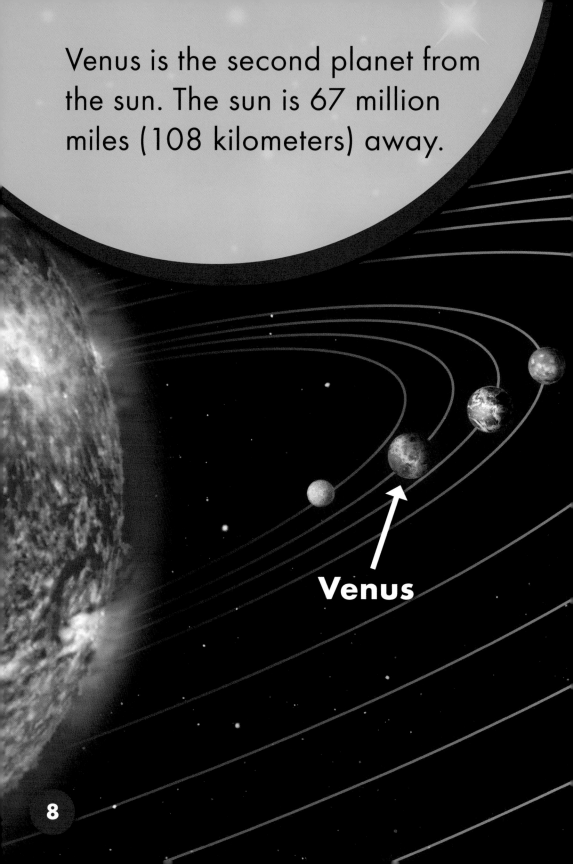

Venus is the second planet from the sun. The sun is 67 million miles (108 kilometers) away.

Venus

Venus and the other planets **orbit** the sun. The sun's **gravity** pulls on the planets to keep them from moving away.

A year is the time it takes a planet to travel once around the sun. A year on Venus equals 225 Earth days.

A day is the time it takes a planet to spin once on its **axis**. A day on Venus equals 243 Earth days. A day on Venus is longer than a year on Venus!

axis

Venus has the hottest surface of any planet in the **solar system**. Its **atmosphere** is made of gases that trap heat on the planet's surface.

The temperature there is about 870° Fahrenheit (465° Celsius). Metal would melt on the surface.

Clouds made of **sulfuric acid** move quickly across the sky. **Acid rain** falls from the clouds. It dries up before it reaches the land.

Volcanoes shaped much of the land on Venus. **Lava** blasted out of the volcanoes millions of years ago.

The lava flowed over the land and hardened into smooth, flat plains.

Hardened bubbles of lava made flat-topped hills. Some bubbles broke and made spider-web patterns on the land.

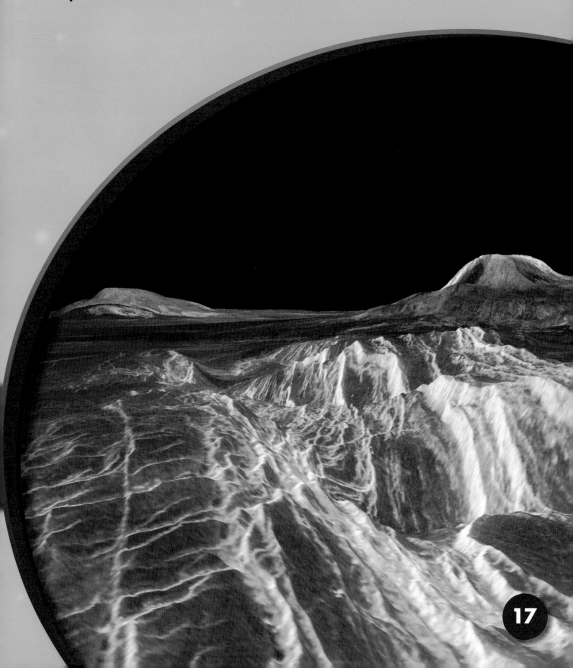

Maxwell Montes

Venus has several
mountain ranges.
Maxwell Montes
is the tallest peak.
It stands nearly 7
miles (11 kilometers)
high!

Deep **canyons** cross the land in some places. Venus also has bowl-shaped holes called **craters**.

The atmosphere around Venus makes the planet's surface hard to see. Scientists are sending **space probes** there to gather information.

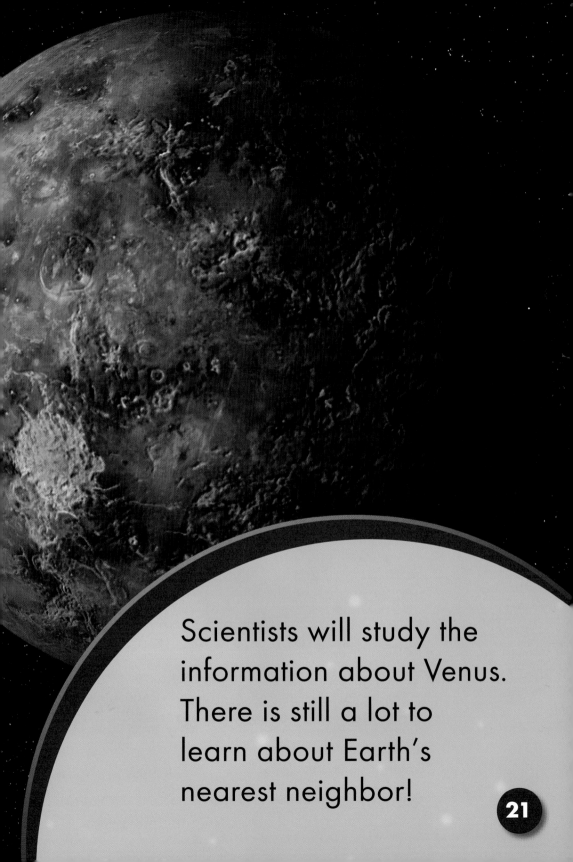

Scientists will study the
information about Venus.
There is still a lot to
learn about Earth's
nearest neighbor!

Glossary

acid rain—droplets of acid mixed with droplets of other gases that fall from clouds

atmosphere—the gases around an object in space

axis—an imaginary line that runs through the center of a planet; a planet spins on its axis.

canyons—deep, narrow valleys

craters—holes made when meteorites or other space objects crash into moons, planets, or other objects

gravity—the force that pulls objects toward each other; gravity keeps objects from moving away into space.

lava—melted rock; lava can harden into different land forms when it cools.

orbit—to travel around an object in space; Venus has an orbit that is almost a perfect circle.

planet—a large, round space object that orbits the sun and is alone in its orbit

Roman goddess—a female god worshipped by the people of ancient Rome

solar system—the sun and the objects that orbit it; the solar system has planets, moons, comets, and asteroids.

space probes—spacecraft that explore planets and other space objects and send information back to Earth; space probes do not carry people.

sulfuric acid—a type of matter that eats away at anything it touches

volcanoes—holes in a planet's surface that lava flows out of; over time, the lava can form a mountain.

To Learn More

AT THE LIBRARY

Landau, Elaine. *Venus*. New York, N.Y.: Children's Press, 2008.

Mist, Rosalind. *Mercury and Venus*. Mankato, Minn.: QEB Publishing, 2009.

Wimmer, Teresa. *Venus*. Mankato, Minn.: Creative Education, 2008.

ON THE WEB

Learning more about Venus is as easy as 1, 2, 3.

1. Go to www.factsurfer.com.

2. Enter "Venus" into the search box.

3. Click the "Surf" button and you will see a list of related Web sites.

With factsurfer.com, finding more information is just a click away.

BLASTOFF! JIMMY CHALLENGE

Blastoff! Jimmy is hidden somewhere in this book. Can you find him? If you need help, you can find a hint at the bottom of page 24.

Index

Blastoff! Jimmy Challenge (from page 23).
Hint: Go to page 18 and take a "peak."